A P A T H Y

A LIFE CHOICE

ROB TOBIN

SUMMERSDALE

Summersdale Publishers Ltd
46 West Street
Chichester
West Sussex
PO19 1RP
UK

www.summersdale.com

Printed in Denmark by
Nørhaven Paperback A/S, Viborg

Introduction

According to Oscar Wilde, a cynic is 'A man who knows the price of everything and the value of nothing', which is a refreshing antidote to the feel-good, be calm, de-stress and motivational trends that have crept into our society in recent years.

It wasn't always like this. In past centuries people would look at the world through grey-tinted spectacles. So what better way to combat the nicey nicey nineties than with this treasure trove of the world's finest cynical and defeatest quotations?

A LIFe CHOICe

If you live long enough,
you'll see that
every victory turns
into a defeat.

Simone de Beavoir
Touts les hommes sont mortels

A PATHY

I want to be bored to death,
as good a way to go as any.

Peter De Vries
Comfort me with Apples

A LIFE CHOICE

Other people are
quite dreadful.
The only possible
society is oneself.

Oscar Wilde
An Ideal Husband

APATHY

I get my exercise acting
as a pall bearer
to my friends who exercise.

Chauncey Depew

A LIFE CHOICE

Happy is the man with a
wife to tell him
what to do and a
secretary to do it.

Lord Mancroft
Observer, "Sayings of the Week" 18 Dec 1966

A PATHY

Alas! The hours we
waste in work
and similar inconsequence,
Friends, I beg you
do not shirk
Your daily task of indolence.

Don Marquis
The Almost Perfect State

A LIFe CHOICe

It is better to have
loafed and lost
than never to have
loafed at all.

James Thurber
Fables for Our Time, "The Courtship of All"

A P A T H Y

'Tis the voice of the sluggard,
I hear him complain;
"You have waked me too
soon, I must slumber again".

Isaac Watts
The Sluggard

A LIFE CHOICE

I am happiest when I am idle. I could live for months without performing any kind of labour, and at the expiration of that time I should feel fresh and vigorous enough to go right on in the same time for numerous more months.

Artemus Ward
Pyrotechny

A PATHY

It was such a lovely day
I thought it was a
pity to get up.

W. Somerset Maugham
Our Betters

I enjoy convalescence. It is
the part that makes the
illness worthwhile.

George Bernard Shaw
Back to Methuselah

APATHY

I am interested in leisure in the way a poor man is interested in money. I can't get enough of it.

Attributed to Prince Philip

A LIFE CHOICE

The wisdom of a learned
man cometh by
opportunity of leisure: and he
that hath little
business shall become wise.

Bible
Ecclesiastes 38. 24-25

A P A T H Y

You should do nothing that did not absolutely please you. Be idle, be very idle! The habits of your mind are such that you will necessarily do much; but be as idle as you can.

S.T. Coleridge
Letter to Southey

A LIFE CHOICE

Every man is, or hopes
to be, an Idler

Samuel Johnson
The Idler

A PATHY

I am sure that indolence –
indefeasible indolence –
is the true state of man,
and business
the invention of
the old Teazer.

Charles Lamb
Letter to Wordsworth, 1805

A LIFE CHOICE

There is one piece of advice, in a life of study, which I think no one will object to; and that is, every now and then to be completely idle, – to do nothing at all.

Sydney Smith
Sketches of Moral Philosophy

A P A T H Y

Increased means and
increased leisure
are the two civilisers of men.

Benjamin Disraeli
*Speech to Conservatives of Manchester,
3 April 1872*

A LIFE CHOICE

Leisure is the mother
of Philosophy.

Thomas Hobbes
Leviathan *iv, 46*

APA/HY

Leisure is the best of all
possessions.

Socrates
Diogenes Laertius

There is no pleasure in
having nothing to do;
the fun is having lots to do
and not doing it.

Mary Wilson Little

A P A T H Y

What's wrong with
dropping out?
To me, this is the whole
point: one's right
to withdraw from a social
environment that
offers no spiritual
sustenance, and to
mind one's own business.

William S Burroughs

A LIFE CHOICE

One little chore to do, one little commission to fulfil, one message to carry, would spoil heaven itself.

Henry D Thoreau
Journal, 21 July 1851

APATHY

So that what was indolence
was called wisdom.

Tacitus

A LIFE CHOICE

I have spent my life
laboriously doing nothing.

Grotius

A PATHY

With ecstasies so sweet
As none can ever guess
Who walk not with the feet
Of joy in idleness

Robert Bridges
Spring

That indolent but delightful
condition of doing nothing.

Pliny the Younger

APATHY

Better to idle well than
work badly.

Spanish proverb

A LIFE CHOICE

Serious matters can wait
until tomorrow.

Cornelius Nepos
Pelopidas

APATHY

To do nothing is in every man's power.

Samuel Johnson
The Rambler

A LIFE CHOICE

Procrastination
– the art of keeping up with
yesterday.

Don Marquis

A P A T H Y

Never put off until tomorrow
what you can
do the day after tomorrow
just as well.

Mark Twain
The Late Benjamin Franklin

A LIFE CHOICE

Work is the refuge of
people who have
nothing better to do.

Oscar Wilde

APATHY

. . . saves time like putting off
until tomorrow
what you should do today.

Malcolm Muggeridge

My father taught me to work, but not to love it. I never did like to work, and I don't deny it. I'd rather read, tell stories, crack jokes, talk, laugh – anything but work.

Abraham Lincoln

A PATHY

The chief attraction of military service has consisted and will consist in this compulsory and irreproachable idleness.

Tolstoy
War and Peace

Put off the evil hour as
long as you can.

Proverb

APATHY

As peace is the end of war,
so to be idle is
the ultimate purpose
of the busy.

Samuel Johnson
The Idler

He that knows nothing,
doubts nothing.

Proverb

APATHY

Hard work has never killed
anyone, but it frightens some
people half to death.

Aldous Huxley

A LIFE CHOICE

Marriage has many pains
but celibacy has no
pleasures.

Samuel Johnson
Rasselas

A P A T H Y

If it rained knowledge, I'd
hold out my hand;
but I would not give myself
the trouble
to go in quest of it.

Boswell
Life of Johnson

A LIFE CHOICE

In this world nothing can be
said to be certain,
except death and taxes.

Benjamin Franklin
letter to Jean-Baptiste Le Roy

A P A T H Y

Cheer up, the worst is
yet to come.

Philander Johnson
Shooting Stars

A LIFE CHOICE

Thank heaven the sun
has gone in,
and I don't have to go out
and enjoy it.

Logan Pearsall Smith

APATHY

Call no man happy
until he dies,
he is at best fortunate.

Plutarch
Solon

It is unfortunate, considering
enthusiasm
moves the world, that
so few enthusiasts
can be trusted to
speak the truth.

A. J. Balfour

APATHY

Marriage is a romance
in which the hero
dies in the first chapter.

Anon
Quoted by Barbara Gourdy
– Falling Angels

Like every man of sense and
good feeling,
I abominate work.

Aldous Huxley

APATHY

The lecture theatre – the place where information passes from the notebook of the lecturer to the notebook of the student without necessarily passing throught the mind of either.

Jim White

A LIFE CHOICE

Mother is the dead heart of
the family, spending
father's earnings on
consumer goods to enhance
the environment in which he
eats, sleeps and
watches the television.

Germaine Greer
The Female Eunuch

APATHY

Brigands demand your
money or your life;
women require both.

Samuel Butler

A LIFE CHOICE

By working faithfully eight
hours a day,
you may eventually get
to be a boss
and work twelve hours a day.

Robert Frost

APATHY

Life is too short to do
anything for oneself
that one can pay others to do
for one.

W. Somerset Maughan
The Summing Up

A LIFE CHOICE

They say hard work never
hurt anybody,
but I figure: why take
the chance?

Ronald Reagan

APATHY

If I were a medical man, I
should prescribe a
holiday to any patient who
considered
his work important.

Bertrand Russell
Autobiography

A LIFE CHOICE

I love mankind
– it's people I can't stand.

Charles M Schultz
Go Fly a Kite, Charlie Brown

APATHY

I never found the companion
that was so companionable
as solitude.

Henry David Thoreau
Solitude

The majority of men devote
the greater part
of their lives to making their
remaining years unhappy.

Jean De La Bruyère

A PATHY

He that lives upon hope
will die fasting.

Benjamin Franklin
Poor Richard's Almanac

A LIFE CHOICE

If people really liked to work,
we'd still be ploughing the
land with
sticks and transporting
goods on our backs.

William Feather

A P A T H Y

Time you can enjoy wasting
is never wasted time.

Anon

A LIFE CHOICE

There are only three events in
a man's life;
birth, life and death; he is not
conscious of
being born, he dies in pain
and he forgets to live.

Jean De La Bruyère

A PATHY

Ours is a world where people
don't know
what they want and are
willing to go
through hell to get it.

Don Marquis

A LIFE CHOICE

Laziness implies a lot of intelligence. It is the normal healthy attitude of a man with nothing to do.

Sir Heneage Oglivie

A PATHY

Anybody who works is a fool.
I don't work,
I merely inflict myself
on the public.

Robert Morley

Work is the only dirty
four-letter
word in the language.

Abbie Hoffman
Harpers Magazine, 1970

A PATHY

You marry the man of your
dreams, ladies,
but 14 years later you're
married to a couch
that burps.

Roseanne Barr
Roseanne, 1986

A LIFE CHOICE

It's always been and always
will be the
same in the world: the horse
does the work
and the coachman is tipped.

Anon

A PATHY

People would rather sleep
their way through life
than stay awake for it.

Edward Albee

A LIFE CHOICE

Life is a concentration camp.
You're stuck here and there's
no way out
and you can only rage
impotently
against your persecutors.

Woody Allen
Esquire, 1977

A PATHY

Life is a practical joke.

Paul Bocuse

A LIFE CHOICE

Life is a shit sandwich and
everyday you take
another bite.

Joe Schmidt

A PATHY

Life's a piece of shit,
when you look at it.

Eric Idle
Life Of Brian

A LIFE CHOICE

There is only the difference
of a letter between the
beginning and the end of life
- creation and cremation.

Sir Herbert Beerbohm Tree

A P A T H Y

Lord Illingworth:
The Book of Life begins
with a man
and a woman in a garden.

Mrs Allonby:
It ends with Revelations.

Oscar Wilde
A Woman of No Importance

The shorter the hours, the larger the income. Don't get into the habit of putting in long hours or you may be set down into a permanent subordinate position.

George Ade
Fables

A PATHY

His sole concern with
work was
considering how he might
best avoid it.

Anatole France
Revolt of the Angels

Work is the scythe of time.

Napoleon Bonaparte, 1815

A PATHY

Set me anything to do
as a task, and it is
inconceivable the desire I
have to do something else.

George Bernard Shaw

A LIFE CHOICE

It is easier to admire
hardwork if you don't do it.

Unknown
Meditations on Wall Street.

A P A T H Y

Work is the curse of the
drinking classes.

Oscar Wilde

A LIFE CHOICE

Life is a one way street.

Bernard Berenson
Notes, 1950

APATHY

All of the animals excepting
man know that
the principal business of life
is to enjoy it.

Samuel Butler
Notebooks

A LIFE CHOICE

We are but tenants, and ...
shortly the great Landlord will
give us notice that our lease
has expired.

Joseph Jefferson
Inscription on his monument

A PATHY

He beats the bush and
another catches the bird.

Old French Proverb

A LIFE CHOICE

It is not necessary that a man should earn his living by the sweat of his brow, unless he sweats easier than I do.

Henry D Thoreau

A P A T H Y

The brain is a
wonderful organ.
It starts working the moment
you get up,
and does not stop until you
get into the office.

Attributed to Robert Frost

94

A LIFE CHOICE

In a hierarchy every
employee tends to rise
to his level of incompetence.

Laurence J. Peter
The Peter Principle

APATHY

One should not exaggerate
the importance of trifles.
Life, for instance, is much
too short to be taken
seriously.

Attributed to Nicolas Bentley

A LIFe CHOICe

Living is a sickness from which sleep provides relief every sixteen hours.   [...] The Remedy is Death.

Nicolas Chamfort

A P A T H Y

Thirty million, mostly fools.
[When asked the population of England]

Thomas Carlyle

A LIFE CHOICE

Life is just one damned thing
after another.

Elbert Hubbard
A Thousand and One Epigrams

A PATHY

Life is as tedious as a
twice-told tale
Vexing the dull ear of a
drowsy man.

William Shakespeare
King John

A LIFE CHOICE

It is better to be a fool
than to be dead.

R L Stevenson

APATHY

Friendship is a disinterested
commerce between equals;
love an abject intercourse
between tyrants and slaves.

Oliver Goldsmith

Work is accomplished by
those employees who
have not yet reached their
level of incompetence.

Laurence J Peter
The Peter Principle

APATHY

Life is a tragedy when
seen in close-up,
but a comedy in long-shot.

Charlie Chaplin

A LIFE CHOICE

Life is a jest; and all
things show it.
I thought so once but
now I know it.

John Gay
My Own Epitaph

APATHY

Life is one long process
of getting tired.

Samuel Butler

A LIFE CHOICE

Life would be tolerably
agreeable if it
were not for its
amusements.

Edward Bulwer-Lytton

APATHY

The basic fact about
human existence
is not that it is a tragedy, but
that it is a bore.

H. L. Mencken
Prejudices

A LIFE CHOICE

I do not want people to be
very agreeable, as it saves
me the trouble of liking them
a great deal.

Jane Austen
Letters

A PATHY

I have often thought
upon death,
and I find it the least
of all evils.

Francis Bacon
An Essay Upon Death

A LIFE CHOICE

Never, ever, bloody
anything ever.

Rick Mayall
Mr Jolly Lives Next Door

A PATHY

A person seldom falls sick,
but the bystanders are
animated with a faint hope
that he will die.

Ralph Waldo Emerson

A LIFE CHOICE

I hate quotations.

Ralph Waldo Emerson

A PATHY

If all the year were
playing holidays,
To sport would be as tedious
as to work;
But when they seldom come,
they wish'd for come.

William Shakespeare
Henry IV

A LIFE CHOICE

Who first invented Work–and
tied the free
And holy-day rejoicing
spirit down
To the ever-haunting
importunity
Of business, in the green
fields, and the town–
To plough–loom–anvil–
spade–and, oh, most sad,
To this dry drudgery of
desk's dead wood?

Charles Lamb
Letter to Barton

APATHY

He may live without books, –
what is knowledge
but grieving?
He may live without hope, –
what is hope but deceiving?
He may live without love, –
what is passion but pining?
But where is the man that
can live without dining?

Owen Meredith
Lucille

A LIFE CHOICE

Man, I can assure you,
is a nasty creature.

Molière

A PATHY

The ceaseless labour of
your life is to
build the house of
your death.

Montaigne

A LIFE CHOICE

If one judges love by the
majority of its effects, it is
more like hatred than
like friendship.

Duc de la Rochefoucauld

A PATHY

If you give me six lines
written by the most honest
man, I will find something in
them to hang him.

Attributed to Cardinal Richelieu

A LIFE CHOICE

The world itself is but a
large prison,
out of which some are
daily led to execution.

Sir Walter Raleigh

A P A T H Y

'Blessed is the man who expects nothing, for he shall never be disappointed' was the ninth beatitude.

Alexander Pope
Letter to Fortescue

A LIFE CHOICE

In the misfortunes of our
best friends we
find something that is not
unpleasing.

Duc De La Rochefoucauld

A PATHY

So little done, so much to do.

Cecil Rhodes
[Last words]

A LIFE CHOICE

The crash of the whole solar
and stellar systems
could only kill you once.

Thomas Carlyle
Letter

**For the latest humour books
from Summersdale, check out**

www.summersdale.com